5/05

real U

GUIDE TO

SAVING
AND INVESTING

MIKE KAVANAGH, CFP®

Real U Guides

Publisher and CEO:
Steve Schultz

Editor-in-Chief:
Megan Stine

Art Director:
C.C. Krohne

Illustration:
Mike Strong

Production Manager:
Alice Todd

Associate Editor:
Steve Otfinoski

Editorial Assistant:
Cody O. Stine

Copy Editor:
Leslie Fears

Library of Congress Control Number: 2004090627

ISBN: 0-9744159-3-6

10 9 8 7 6 5 4 3 2

Published by
Real U, Inc.
2582 Centerville Rosebud Rd.
Loganville, GA 30052

www.realuguides.com

Real U is a registered trademark of Real U, Inc.

Photo Credits:
Cover and Page 1: Javier Pierini/Getty Images; Page 3:
Digital Vision/Getty Images; Page 4: Janis Christie/Getty
Images; Page 5: Woman on bed with scarf, Trinette Reed/Getty
Images; Stacks of money, Photodisc Collection/Getty Images;
Composite of woman and stock charts, Chad Baker/Ryan
McVay/Getty Images; Graduates, Digital Vision/Getty Images;
Retired couple with bikes, PhotoLink/Getty Images; Page 6:
Digital Vision/Getty Images; Page 7: Friends pouring cham-
pagne, Digital Vision/Getty Images; Slot machine, ArtToday;
Page 8: Young girl at computer, Scott T Baxter/Getty Images;
Woman in CD store, ArtToday; Page 9: Jim Arbogast/Getty
Images; Page 10: Ryan McVay/Getty Images; Page 11:
PhotoLink/Getty Images; Page 12: ArtToday; Page 13:
ArtToday; Page 14: ArtToday; Page 15: Trinette Reed/Getty
Images; Page 16: Chad Baker/Getty Images; Page 17: Photodisc
Collection/Getty Images; Page 18: ArtToday; Page 19: Ryan
McVay/Getty Images; Page 20: ArtToday; Page 21: Andreas
Pollok/Getty Images; Page 22: Gold ingot, Photodisc
Collection/Getty Images; Collectible car, ArtToday/Getty
Images; Page 23: Aerial view of subdivision, PhotoLink/Getty
Images; House with pool, SW Productions/Getty Images;
Page 24: Javier Pierini/Getty Images; Page 25: Investment
montage, Photodisc Collection/Getty Images; Man on sofa,
Megan Stine; Page 26: Paul Vozdic/Getty Images; Page 27:
ArtToday; Page 28: ArtToday; Page 29: ArtToday; Page 30:
ArtToday; Page 33: ArtToday; Page 34: ArtToday; Page 35:
Chad Baker/Ryan McVay/Getty Images; Page 36: ArtToday;
Page 37: ArtToday; Page 38: Ryan McVay/Getty Images;
Page 39: Don Farrall/Getty Images; Page 40: Comstock
Images/Getty Images; Page 42: ArtToday; Page 43: Stock
certificates, PhotoLink/Getty Images; Girl on bike, ArtToday;
Page 44: ArtToday; Page 45: Javier Pierini/Getty Images;
Page 46: Bonds chart in newspaper, ArtToday; Skyscrapers,
PhotoLink/Getty Images; Page 47: ArtToday; Page 48: Pando
Halll/Getty Images; Page 49: Photodisc Collection/Getty
Images; Page 50: PhotoLink/Getty Images; Page 51: Digital
Vision/Getty Images; Page 52: Photodisc Collection/Getty
Images; Page 53: Photodisc Collection/Getty Images;
Page 54: ArtToday; Page 57: Man at home, Digital
Vision/Getty Images; Woman in deck chair, Michael
Matisse/Getty Images; Page 58: PhotoLink/Getty Images;
Page 59: Monica Lau/Getty Images; Page 60: Doug
Menuez/Getty Images; Page 61: Ron Chapple/Getty Images;
Page 62: Digital Vision/Getty Images; Page 63: Geoff
Manasse/Getty Images; Back Cover: Pando Hall/Getty Images.

Funding for this grant was awarded by the Illinois State Library (ISL), a Division of the Office of Secretary of State, using funds provided by the Institute of Museum and Library Services (IMLS), under the federal Library Services and Technology (LSTA).

realU®

GUIDE TO

SAVING AND INVESTING

MIKE KAVANAGH, CFP®

Everyone's doing it...

Tell the truth: you were shocked to find out that your spinster aunt, your plumber, your dental hygienist, and your best friend had all invested in the stock market long before you. Or maybe you weren't shocked —just jealous. Maybe you've been wanting to get in on the action just like everyone else, but you didn't know how or where to start.

Whether you've already taken the plunge by investing in a 401(k) at work—or you have no idea what that is and you're totally green when it comes to stocks, bonds, and mutual funds (which isn't a bad color, since we're talking money)—we've got some great advice and simple definitions to help you get started investing like a pro.

So turn the page and check out our insider's tips—straight from a CERTIFIED FINANCIAL PLANNER™—on everything you need to know to open a brokerage account, buy stocks and mutual funds, invest for retirement, and much more. And hey—we'll even tell you how to make a million dollars by the time you're 65! With any luck, your dental hygienist will be very jealous.

And welcome to

realU

REAL U GUIDE TO SAVING AND INVESTING
TABLE OF CONTENTS

QUIZ:

ARE YOU A HOPELESS SPENDTHRIFT OR AN INVESTMENT WHIZ KID?

Saving and investing are fun! Also fun: shopping, spending, eating out, not thinking about your financial future, cashing your paycheck, and hitting the clubs with your credit card and a few friends.

The thing is, one of these kinds of fun will leave you with a nice fat nest egg when you retire, while the other will simply leave you with a lot of clothes that are out of style. Take this quiz to find out if you've got investment smarts—or if you'll just be saying "That smarts!" when your lousy investments come back to bite you.

I got a raise!

1.

For some reason, your boss just gave you a sweet little raise at work, so now you're bringing home an extra $30 a week. What are you going to do with the money?

A. What do you mean "bringing home"? If you're lucky, those 30 bucks will cover dinner and drinks with your friends on the way home. (Maybe you'll invite your boss to join the celebration.)

B. Invest it...in a totally new wardrobe! (Maybe your boss will give you another raise when he sees your new threads.)

C. Invest it...in investments. (Maybe someday your boss will be working for you!)

2.

Although you'd rather not divulge too much about your retirement plan, let's just say it...

A. Offers excellent back support and a pillow-top.

B. Involves the lottery and a very successful trip to Vegas.

C. Is so good, it puts your own broker's plan to shame.

your retirement plan?

starting early...

4.

You understand investing terminology—no problem. When your financial advisor tells you to get a diverse portfolio, you pick up:

A. Some Pixies, a baroque cello concerto, Miles Davis's "Sketches of Spain," Britney Spears's newest single, and Tom Jones's greatest hits.

B. A blonde, a brunette, and a redhead.

C. A wide range of investments, including some blue chip stocks, some mutual funds, and some stocks you've hand-picked yourself.

3.

Everyone says you should start saving early, but what's your idea of early?

A. Before you start driving a minivan to ballet recitals, watching Oprah, and packing lunches that involve fruit snacks.

B. Before you start driving a motorized wheelchair around the supermarket, watching *Jeopardy*, and making lunches that involve prunes and apple sauce.

C. Before you start driving.

Investing is all about waiting. How long can you wait?

5.

Investing is all about waiting, but that's no problem for you. After all, the longest you've ever waited for something is:

A. 47 minutes—the time it took for your Spaghetti Bolognese to arrive when you went out to dinner the other night. (And you left a measly tip to let the waiter know how you felt about it, too!)

B. 17 days—the time it took your ex to realize what a mistake she'd made and come back to you.

C. 2 years, 3 months, and 21 days— the time it took your dad to break down and finally let you drive his Corvette.

SCORING

Remember when your kindergarten teachers told you there were no wrong answers? They were lying. The right answers are C. Give yourself one point for every right answer.

4-5 Points:
Nice work. You're certainly not a hopeless wastrel, and may be well on your way to becoming an investment guru. Of course, if you were really smart, you would have dumped that tanking tech stock instead of taking this quiz.

2-4 Points:
All right, wise guy—sounds like you know just enough about investing to get yourself in trouble. Never fear—this guide has everything you need to know to avoid embarrassment and get ahead at investing.

0-2 Points:
Ouch. Turn the page. Read. Please. And keep your checkbook out of reach until you finish this book.

←a diverse portfolio?

Saving is an absolutely necessary piece of the saving and investing puzzle.

PIGGY BANKS:
SAVING 101

Okay, we admit it. There are two key words in the title of this book, and saving isn't the sexy one.

By comparison to the thrill ride of investing your money in the stock market and watching it climb, saving seems like the kiddie cars or the bench seat on the carousel. Saving is the dull, quiet cousin you get stuck with at the family reunion when you'd rather be hanging with your hip uncle who drives a Porsche.

But the truth is that there's a lot to be said for saving. For one thing, when you're saving up for something special, every 50 bucks you sock away lets you picture yourself with the reward—tooling around in that new sports car, for instance.

And even when you're not saving for a new toy, hoarding your money produces results that are indisputably positive. Stash away $100 a month for a year and what have you got? You've got at least $1200 you didn't have a year ago. Never mind that you'll also earn a little interest if you put the cash somewhere other than under your mattress.

So read on. Just like at the family reunion, you've got to deal with the quiet cousin sometime—so you might as well get started now.

save for vacations

SAVING AND INVESTING:
WHAT'S THE DIFFERENCE

Let's say you want a new pair of skis for next winter, or a mountain bike for next summer. It's probably not a good idea to invest in the stock market with the hopes that by the time the weather changes, you'll make a killing and can head for the ski slopes or the bike trails.

On the other hand, if you want to accumulate enough money to put your kids through college, you probably want to do something more than just save a few bucks each week and stuff them under the mattress.

In other words, the difference between saving and investing is a matter of goals and time frames. Simply put, you save money for short-term goals and low-ticket items. You invest it for long-term goals and high-ticket items. For example:

You SAVE for...	Time frame for saving
Vacation cruise	six months
New car	one year
Emergency or Rainy Day Fund	one to two years

You INVEST for...	Time frame for investing
Down payment on your dream house	five years
Your child's college education	15-20 years
Your retirement in sunny California, Florida, or the South of France	30-40 years

The most important thing to remember about saving and investing is this: You should save before you invest. It makes no sense to put money into a retirement account if you don't have a nice cushion in the bank for dealing with emergencies.

invest for long-term goals

ABOUT THE RAINY DAY FUND

Putting money away for a rainy day is something of a given—and it's the very first thing you should save for. Face it: An unexpected blow to your bank account—like losing your job, being disabled, or some other catastrophe—could change your life dramatically if you're not prepared. Most financial experts say your rainy day fund should be equal to three to six months of your living expenses, including rent or mortgage, utilities, car payment, and groceries. That might seem like a lot of money, but it won't if you lose your job and have to live on it until you find work.

BEFORE YOU SAVE—INSURE!

Don't even say it—we know what you're thinking. Who wants to spend money on something as boring as insurance if you don't have to? It's hard enough to give up things like new clothes, movies, or dinners with friends in order to put money in the bank for the future or a rainy day. But putting your hard earned cash into insurance—when all get for it is a piece of paper you hope never to use—feels like you're just digging a hole and pouring money into the ground, never to be seen again.

But that's the deal—that's what you've got to do if you want to protect your lifestyle. Some kinds of insurance are required by law—auto insurance, for example—and you probably already have that. Here's a quick look at the other kinds of insurance you can purchase, and why they're a good idea.

HOMEOWNER'S INSURANCE

This protects your home from theft, vandalism, fire, and other unforeseen disasters. The bank will require it if you have a mortgage. If you rent, renter's insurance is also available and will protect your stuff from the same kinds of bad-news events.

HEALTH AND DISABILITY INSURANCE

If you work for a company or business, health insurance may be provided by your employer, but many small companies do not provide benefits. You should seriously consider buying your own health and disability insurance if you aren't covered at work. According to the National Association of Life Underwriters, three out of ten working people between ages 35 and 65 will become disabled for 90 days or more and nearly one in five will become disabled for five years or more.

AUTO INSURANCE

It's required—at least liability coverage is—if you want to drive a car you own. The more money you make and the more assets you have as time goes by, the higher the liability coverage you should carry. Why? Because if you injure someone in an accident, you can be sued personally for all you're worth. The more you're worth, the more you have to lose.

LIFE INSURANCE

You probably don't need life insurance while you're single, but as soon as you're married—and definitely when you have children—you'll want to buy a life insurance policy to provide your family and other dependents with money to live on in case you die. How much? A good rule of thumb is to buy five times your salary in life insurance. That sounds like a lot of money, but if you buy term insurance, which is renewed after a year or other term of time, it's surprisingly affordable. If you can't spring for that much, at least buy a policy that will cover your salary times two.

HOW AND WHERE TO SAVE:

SOME GREAT AND NOT-SO-GREAT PLACES TO PUT YOUR MONEY

That rainy day fund you're trying to accumulate, or the money you're saving for a big trip to Hawaii, needs to go somewhere safe.

You don't want to take any risks with this ka-ching, because you've got plans to use it, right? So money that's ear-marked as "savings" should not go into a hot stock tip—or on red at your local casino.

On the other hand, you don't want to just stick it into an account where you're earning something like .000000025 interest, either. That's diddly-squat. You want the money you save to grow, no matter how soon you might need it. After all—earning interest on money that's just sitting there is the easiest money you'll ever make.

So where should you put your cash? From worst to first, here are the choices:

CHECKING ACCOUNT

A terrible savings choice for two reasons: One, you'll be tempted to spend it because it's readily available. Two, most banks stopped paying interest on checking accounts a long time ago, or if they're still paying it, the amount is minimal. Your growth potential here isn't much better than hiding your money under the mattress.

SAVINGS ACCOUNT

A little better, but not much. The one good thing about savings accounts is the psychological effect: You won't be as tempted to spend the money because it's more difficult to get it out. But the interest you'll earn is so slight, it's hardly worth it.

MONEY MARKET ACCOUNT OR FUND

A definite improvement in terms of interest rates, but that's not the whole story. A money market account is sort of like a cross between a checking account and a savings account. Often, you can write checks against the money in your account, but there's a minimum dollar amount—$500, for instance—so you can't use it to pay the phone bill (unless you have a monster phone bill because you're constantly on the cell to your girlfriend in Thailand). Sometimes there's a limit on the number of transactions (withdrawals or transfers) you can make each month as well. Banks offer money market accounts, and brokerage firms offer something similar called money market funds. There are a few small differences, but basically they're the same thing.

In the banking world, CD's are Certificates of Deposit, which you can buy from a bank or other financial institution.

Your growth potential in a checking account isn't much better than hiding your money under the mattress.

you're going to be hit by a whopping penalty which will probably wipe out the interest you earned and then some. If you buy a CD, be sure this is money you won't be needing anytime soon.

U.S. SAVING BONDS

A savings bond is an investment you make in the federal government. What you are doing when you buy a savings bond is lending the government your money. When you cash in the bond, you get back the money you lent—which is called your principal—plus interest. If you buy the EE savings bond, you get a bond certificate for which you pay half the face value. A $100 EE bond, for example, will cost you $50. The EE bond has a guaranteed time period (currently 20 years) in which it matures, or reaches full value. In this regard, it is similar to a CD. But there are some definite advantages to a savings bond. You pay no state or local income taxes on the interest you earn on a bond and you only pay the federal taxes when you cash it in. The Series I bonds match inflation, the increase in the cost of living in the economy. The series EE bonds go up and down with other interest rates. A savings bond can't be cashed in for 12 months, and there is a small penalty of your last three months of interest if you cash it in during the first 5 years. Buy them online at www.treasurydirect.gov.

CD'S

Yes, we know. You'd love to put all your extra dough into those shiny little plastic disks that play music. In the banking world, however, CD's are Certificates of Deposit, which you can buy from a bank or other financial institution. Here's how it works: You agree to let the bank have your money for three months or longer. Because you're tying up your money for a specific period of time, the interest rates for a CD are generally higher than either savings accounts or money market funds. The longer the time period, the higher the interest rate. But here's the catch. If you take out the money before the time period is up,

DOES IT PAY TO SAVE?

**No matter where you decide to save your money,
if you're getting interest on your deposit it's going to add up.**

How fast it multiplies depends on the interest rate. The table below shows how a monthly deposit of $100 grows over a period of years. Before you get too excited about these numbers, however, remember: In this economy, as of 2004, you're not likely to get an interest rate anywhere near 4% on a savings account. (But you can do even better than that in the stock market—possibly averaging 7, 8, or 9 percent return on your investment over a period of years—which is why you'll want to check out the investing chapter on Page 19.)

The following chart shows how a monthly deposit of $100 grows over a period of years. Compounding is monthly, and deposits are made at the beginning of the period.

INTEREST RATE (%)	5 YEARS	10 YEARS	15 YEARS	20 YEARS	25 YEARS	30 YEARS
1.5	6,234	12,954	20,197	28,003	36,418	45,487
2.0	6,315	13,294	21,006	29,529	38,947	49,355
2.5	6,397	13,646	21,858	31,162	41,704	53,648
3.0	6,481	14,009	22,754	32,912	44,712	58,419
3.5	6,566	14,385	23,698	34,788	47,996	63,727
4.0	6,652	14,774	24,691	36,800	51,584	69,636
4.5	6,740	15,177	25,738	38,958	55,507	76,223
5.0	6,829	15,593	26,840	41,275	59,799	83,573
5.5	6,920	16,024	28,002	43,762	64,498	91,780
6.0	7,012	16,470	29,227	46,435	69,646	100,954
6.5	7,106	16,932	30,519	49,308	75,289	111,217
7.0	7,201	17,409	31,881	52,397	81,480	122,709

THE JOYS OF COMPOUND INTEREST

Why does the money you stash in a bank or other financial institution grow so fast? Two words: compound interest. What this means is that every day your money is in the bank you're earning interest—not only on the original investment, but also on the interest that you've already earned! In other words, you earn interest on the interest…and then you earn interest on the interest on the interest. It just keeps compounding! If you start with a small investment, it may not seem like it amounts to much, but over a long period of time it can really add up. Interest may be compounded daily, quarterly (every three months), or semiannually (every six months). Daily compounding is the best, needless to say. (If you could talk a bank into compounding hourly, you'd be a genius.)

HOW TO DOUBLE YOUR MONEY: THE RULE OF 72

No matter how math-challenged you are, you've got to love a simple math formula that tells you how long it takes to double your money under just about any circumstance (other than at the craps table in Vegas). It's called the Rule of 72 and here's how it works: You take the number 72 and divide it by the interest rate you're earning. The answer is the number of years it will take to double your money.

For example, let's say your grandmother put $10,000 into a stock market fund when you were 7 years old. (More about stock market funds on Page 28.) And let's say the money earned an average annual return or profit of about 10%. According to the rule of 72, you'd double your money in 7.2 years, which means you'd have $20,000 by the time you were 14. If the money kept earning 10%—which isn't farfetched because that's the historical average for investments in the stock market, over a ten-year period—the money would double again in 7.2 years, to $40,000. Then $80,000, and so on. If you left all the money in the account until you were age 57, you'd be a millionaire! (Thanks, Grandma!)

at least the money's still at work!

PUT IT ON AUTO-PILOT

Sure, you could make a mental note to take out a set amount from your paycheck every two weeks and put it away in a savings account. But what if you "forget"? (Kind of like you "forget" to go on a diet, call your grandmother, or have your teeth cleaned once a year.) It's way too easy to spend loose cash on impulse before you can make it to the bank. So if you're serious about saving, go for the automatic option and sign up to have a designated amount of money pulled out of your checking account once a month before you even see it. The U.S. Savings Bond program has an automatic savings feature that you can check out on the web at www.treasurydirect.gov. For links to other money market funds that offer this service, visit www.realuguides.com.

INVESTING 101:

Investing in stocks can be a crazy risk if you aren't careful... but you can also make more money in stocks, and it should definitely be part of your financial plan.

A REAL U CRASH COURSE

There are three ways to look at investing in the stock market. One: think of it as a gamble that only thrill-seekers or crazy people get involved with. Two: think of it as a way to get rich faster than just about any other form of investing. Three: think of it as a good solid level-headed strategy which any reasonable person would include as part of his or her financial picture.

Well, guess what? All three of those views are correct. Investing in stocks can be a foolhardy crazy risk if you aren't careful...but you can also make more money in stocks...and it should definitely be part of your financial plan, as long as you learn how to follow some rules that will help you steer clear of the insanity and invest wisely.

Investing isn't just about the stock market. There are other places to stash your cash—some much better than others—and we'll give you a quick rundown on all of them in this chapter. But when you think about investing, you should definitely think about stocks first. And when you think about stocks, you should immediately think about mutual funds.

So if you're raring to go, totally psyched, and ready to jump into the stock market with both feet, skip this section and turn to the chapter on mutual funds on Page 27.

On the other hand, if you get nervous when you see the word "crash" in the same headline with the word "investing," you probably need to read on to find out why, statistically, investing in the stock market is one of the smartest things you can do.

WHY INVEST?

The answer to this question is simple. Over the years, investors on average make more money in stocks than in any other form of investment. If you thought the joys of compound interest were fun, and if you were stoked by the Rule of 72, just wait till you take a gander at the kind of profit—what's called the "return on investment"—you can make in the stock market, as compared with other investments. (More about those other kinds of investments later.)

1925-2002

Type of Investment	Average Gain Each Year
STOCKS	10.2%
BONDS	5.5%
TREASURY BILLS	3.8%

Yeah—the stock market was the big winner. Surprised?

Now make no mistake: These numbers are an average. The statistic is based on the stock prices, over time, for the 500 largest companies in the U.S. To get the same results yourself, you would have to invest in those 500 companies equally and steadily over a period of time—usually at least 10 years. If you start picking and choosing individual stocks, or you jump into the market and then jump out again, you may not do so well and you could easily lose a bundle.

There are some simple ways to make sure you do as well as the stock market average as a whole, however, and pull in that 10+%. We'll spell them out carefully in the next few chapters to come.

But first, how about a crash course in the various types of investments that are out there? Whoops—there's that "C" word again. Don't worry—we'll show you how to buckle your seatbelt so you'll have a safe, smooth, and pleasant investing ride.

TYPES OF INVESTMENTS

STOCKS

Stocks are shares in a company or business. Buying stocks means you own part of that company. You buy stock in an individual company because you believe the price or value of the stock will go up over time. You can then sell the stock and spend or invest the profit (which is called "gain"). Some stocks are bought not just with the hope that the price will go up, but because the stock may pay a dividend. When a company does well and makes money, it pays cash dividends to all the shareholders. You can choose to have the dividends reinvested to buy more stock in the company, or you can just take the cash and run. Of course, when the business does poorly, so do you. The value of your shares will go down, and you won't be getting any dividends that period. Stocks are among the most volatile of investments—which means that the value can spike up and then do a death drop that makes the roller coasters at Six Flags look like kiddie rides by comparison—but they can also be the most profitable. When you buy stock, you usually receive a statement indicating the number of shares you own. Very few companies today actually distribute a stock certificate. Read a lot more about stocks starting on Page 37.

our dream house

BONDS

Bonds are basically loans made by individual investors (people) to the city, state, country, or company that issued the bond. When you buy a bond, you're lending money and getting paid interest on your loan. U.S. savings bonds are just one kind of this popular investment. You can also buy bonds from corporations—which means you could own stock in a company, and also buy a bond from the same company. Bonds are usually safer than stocks, but the safety factor depends entirely on who's issuing the bond. U.S. government bonds are very safe. Bonds from a company that makes executive decisions using Tarot cards? Probably less so. As with stocks, when you buy a bond, you will generally receive a statement of the bonds you have purchased. Very few companies or governments issue bond certificates these days. More about bonds starting on Page 45.

MUTUAL FUNDS

A mutual fund is a collection of a variety of different stocks, bonds, or sometimes both, sold under one umbrella name—the name of the mutual fund. When most people say "mutual fund," they're usually talking about a stock fund. This is a popular investment for many middle-income people because it offers a chance to buy a mixture or range of different stocks without having to buy them individually and therefore pay separate fees for each purchase. For more on mutual funds, see Page 27.

REAL ESTATE

Your home is probably the biggest investment you will ever make. It's also your most valuable asset. Homes and other forms of real estate in general tend to go up in value over time and are generally less risky than other kinds of investments. But it's possible to buy a stinker of a house and have a hard time unloading it later. So choose your house wisely, and think about it as part of your financial happiness and well-being. If you're going to invest for profit in other kinds of real estate, such as rental or commercial property, you'd better do your homework. There's no "sure thing" when it comes to investing, and that goes for real estate, too.

When you buy real estate, assuming there is no debt that you owe on the property, you receive a title or deed that shows you own the property.

Anyone who bought a gold bar some years back when it was worth nearly $700 an ounce is now stuck with what may be one of the worst investments in modern times.

GOLD AND SILVER

No matter what you see on the red carpet at awards shows, gold and silver have lost much of their allure in recent times. Anyone who bought a gold bar some years back when it was worth nearly $700 an ounce is now stuck with what may be one of the worst investments in modern times. In 2003, even with a dramatic rise in gold prices in the last several years, an ounce of gold was selling for less than $400 an ounce. That puts the return on gold over 20 years to a whopping negative 40%! Gold is a volatile and risky investment. Silver has an even worse history of pricing. Many financial planners view both these metals as speculative commodities and not a good bet for long-term investment.

GOLD AND SILVER COINS

The hobby aspect of coin collecting makes this an attractive investment for some people, but the value of rare coins fluctuates and is unpredictable over time. Overall, this is a better hobby than an investment.

OTHER COLLECTIBLES AND ANTIQUES

Sorry you let your mom toss out your collection of Brady Bunch drink coasters? Wish you'd held onto your Transformers collection? You might or might not make a killing with these collectibles, depending on what they are and when you try to sell them. Yesterday's junk could be tomorrow's antiques—or vice versa. And that's the problem. Trends change in collectibles. A few years. back trading cards, especially sports cards, were super hot. However, this craze has cooled and many trading card dealers have gone out of business. Like coins, collectibles and antiques are best acquired for the joy they'll bring rather than the possible return on the investment.

Collectibles are best acquired for the joy they'll bring rather than the return on the investment.

great investment!

GETTING REAL ABOUT REAL ESTATE

Real estate can be a valuable investment, but there are some important rules to follow.

RULE #1:

Own your own home first before you starting dabbling in other properties. This may sound silly, but it makes no sense to be a landlord if you are renting yourself.

RULE #2:

Learn as much as you can about the legal and tax implications of owning real estate. These are at least as important as understanding the investment itself. And don't forget that owning property costs money. You'll have to pay taxes, periodic maintenance, and upkeep.

RULE #3:

Be realistic. Don't believe those TV infomercials that say buying real estate today will make you rich tomorrow. It takes time, patience, and knowledge of the market, none of which are easily acquired. Don't get your advice from a book or video some huckster is selling on the tube. Find someone in your community who has succeeded in the real estate market and learn from him or her.

INVESTING PRIORITIES: WHAT TO DO FIRST

Experts agree that your first and most important investment goal should be retirement. If you're young, you may think it's too early to start worrying about that. But the truth is that the sooner you start, the less painful it's going to be because you won't have to fork over as much money each month, and you'll still get the same results.

What about saving for your children's college education, you're thinking? That's number two, for a number of reasons. First, you've only got four years of college to pay for, whereas your retirement years could be several decades, depending on what age you are when you retire and how long you live. And secondly, many experts point out that your children have options to pay for their education—student loans, part-time jobs, scholarships—but no one's going to give you a scholarship for your golden years.

For everything you need to know about investing for retirement, see Page 51.

What about saving for your child's education? That's number two.

Remember: no one's going to give you a scholarship for your retirement.

WHICH INVESTMENTS ARE BEST FOR YOU?

Unlike the question "Why invest?" this one doesn't have an easy answer. Generally speaking, you'll want to invest in a variety of different investments. The fancy term for this is asset allocation, which basically means "don't put all your eggs in one basket." If you allocate your money into a variety of different stocks, bonds, savings accounts and other valuable investments, then you're less likely to lose your shirt when one of them takes a dive and loses value. By owning a home, you are also allocating some of your money into real estate. And because you don't want everything tied up in long-term investments, you should also stick some of your money in short-term savings for emergency use. Get it? Some money here, some money there.

Even when you're just buying one kind of investment—stocks—you'll want to allocate your money to protect yourself from the too-many-eggs-in-one-basket situation. One of the best ways to allocate your money in the stock market is to buy a mutual fund which is, by definition, a big basket of a lot of different stocks. Read on!

Asset allocation basically means "don't put all your eggs in one basket."

diversifying...

CDs

MUTUAL FUN

IRAs

STOCKS

401K

T-BILL

BONDS

MUTUAL FUNDS:

THE BEST WAY TO INVEST

Here it is in a nutshell—the best piece of advice in this entire book. If you want to get the best possible return (or profit) on your investment— and if you want the closest thing you'll ever get to a guarantee that over the long term you'll make money, not lose it—buy an index stock mutual fund.

What's an index fund and how do you go about buying one? We'll define all the terms and spell it out for you in step by step detail on the next few pages. But read carefully before you call a broker or put your money into any investment because not all mutual funds are created equal. And don't even turn the page until you've zeroed in on the one key phrase that is part of this advice: over the long term. We're not talking about making a quick buck here. We're talking about how to take advantage of the fact that in the past 50 years or more, statistics have shown that the stock market as a whole earned a better return on investment than bonds or treasury bills (which are the other two main kinds of investments people are often advised to make).

Wait a minute, you're saying. I want to buy stocks. Yeah, we know, hotshot. You want the thrill of rolling the dice, picking a hot stock, and riding it to double your money in a matter of a few short weeks. Fine—take your vacation money and spend it that way instead of hitting the tables at Vegas. But if you want to see your money grow steadily over time, index mutual funds are the way to go. Read on to find out why!

27

A mutual fund is a collection of stocks that are all lumped together and sold as one package.

When you buy one share of a mutual fund, you're buying ownership in the whole pool of stocks that make up the fund. There might be 20 or 30 stocks in one mutual fund, or there might be 500. Doesn't matter—if you own one share of that fund, you own a tiny piece of each company that's held by the fund.

The good thing about mutual funds is that when you buy one, you're not putting all your eggs in one basket. If one stock in the mutual fund gets hit with some heavy losses, so what? Other stocks can do so well that they offset the losses. Of course, if all the stocks in the fund start to take a dive, look out. You can wind up dropping all of your baskets of eggs, and then you'll end up with an omelet.

There are literally thousands of mutual funds out there, but before you can choose one, you've got to understand the lingo. Here's a glossary of key terms you'll run into, and why they're important.

NO-LOAD FUNDS

A no-load fund is one that charges no commissions or fees for the purchase. You should always look for no-load funds—there's very little reason to pay a fee. (The exception would be if you have a particular interest in a specific fund because it offers a special selection of stocks that you want to invest in.) No-load funds are often sold directly by the company offering them through a web site or toll-free telephone number, or you can buy them from discount brokers. (More about how to open a brokerage account on Page 41.) There is, however, usually an annual maintenance fee of $10 or more for no-load funds—not a big deal, and inexpensive compared to the fees charged with load funds.

LOAD FUNDS

As you might guess, there's a reason why some mutual funds charge a load or fees for the purchase of their shares: They're trying to make money on the deal! But hang on—you're trying to make money from this investment yourself. Oops— conflict of interest. Think twice before paying a load. You'll also notice, if you do some research, that load funds are almost always managed funds as well. We're recommending you stay away from managed funds as you'll see on Page 30.

INDEX

The way people on Wall Street measure the success or failure of any given investment is to ask this question: How did it do compared to the stock market as a whole? And the way they compute how the stock market as a whole is performing is by creating what's called an index. One of the most common indexes is the S&P 500. (S&P stands for Standard &Poor's —an independent company that does the calculations and provides the data.) The S&P 500 is a collection of 500 of the largest companies in America. Any one stock in that group can go up or down on any given day—that's to be expected. But how did the whole collection of 500 stocks do that day? How did they do in a particular week? Or year? When you look at the S&P 500, or another index, you know whether the stock market as a whole is up or down. Investors often ask themselves: How are the stocks I picked doing compared to the index? It's a good question. Most investors have a hard time "beating the market" or doing better than the indexes over a long period of time. (Sure, you might do better than the S&P 500 for a month or even a year, but the odds are against you over the long haul.) That's why buying an index mutual fund makes so much sense. If you can't beat the index, join 'em.

29

Some managed funds will beat the index, but the question is: which ones? If you don't have a crystal ball to predict the answer to that question, you're better off sticking with an index fund.

MANAGED MUTUAL FUNDS

This is the term for mutual funds that are managed, usually just by one individual who makes all the investment decisions —picking and choosing which stocks to buy and which ones to sell, and when to do so. A managed fund may start the year with a specific set of stocks and end the year with a completely different collection of stocks. It's kind of like having just one financial wizard pulling the strings for everyone—and if he or she is good at it, everyone wins. But if the manager stinks, or just gets unlucky, everyone loses. When you buy shares of a managed mutual fund, you're putting all your money into just one person's hands— the manager's. (Some funds are managed by a team of 2 or 3 people, but that's the exception rather than the rule.) Big mutual fund companies such as Fidelity and Vanguard offer managed funds and they compete with each other, hoping that they will produce higher returns than the market average. Studies show that most of them fail to do so over the long term. One reason for this is that their annual expenses are considerably higher than funds that are not managed. Nevertheless, these are the most common and numerous of mutual funds you'll find out there. Our advice is to stay away from managed funds, and stick with an index fund instead.

INDEX MUTUAL FUNDS

Index funds, unlike managed funds, invest in every stock in a particular group or index, such as the S&P 500. Because an index fund is simply trying to "match" the market as a whole, there are very few decisions to be made, and no manager is required. There is also much less buying and selling of different stocks within the fund. Studies show that over a ten-year period or longer, most index funds will do better than most managed mutual funds. Sure, some managed funds will beat the index, but the question is: which ones? If you don't have a crystal ball to predict the answer to that question, you're better off sticking with an index fund. Another plus is that index funds' annual expenses tend to be extremely low.

STOCK MUTUAL FUNDS

These funds own a pool of certain kinds of stocks. Some stock funds are made up entirely of stocks from large companies, so they're called large-cap funds. Funds made up of mid-size or small companies are called mid-cap or small-cap funds. Cap stands for capitalization—a fancy word for "how much money is the company worth?" The number is based on how many shares there are multiplied by the price of a share of stock. A company with a large cap may have 100,000,000 shares at $100 per share, meaning the company has a capitalization of ten billion dollars.

BOND MUTUAL FUNDS

These funds are composed of a pool of specific kinds of bonds, and each fund usually spells out very clearly what type the fund has.

OTHER MUTUAL FUNDS

Funds can be made up of all sorts of investments—real estate, gold, you name it. There are even funds that own a mix of all of the above. They are called balanced funds, total market funds, and many other names.

AGGRESSIVE GROWTH FUNDS

This means the fund manager's goal is to buy stocks that are likely to grow quickly in value. You might think every fund would want that—who wouldn't want their stock prices to rise? But the truth is that there's more risk involved in buying stock in young companies that are growing rapidly (as compared with older, well-established companies that aren't growing so fast, but aren't likely to tank, either). Stocks that might go up quickly have just as much chance of going down. So there's a lot more risk involved in mutual funds that are looking for aggressive growth.

GROWTH FUNDS

Sort of like aggressive growth, but less so. Mutual funds that look for growth are going to take some risk, but not as much as those seeking aggressive growth.

INCOME FUNDS

Funds that are looking for income are basically looking to earn interest from bonds or dividends from stocks. A dividend is money that is paid out, usually four times a year, by a corporation to its stockholders. Dividend income has an advantage in that it is taxed at 15%, which is generally lower than the tax you would pay on bond interest.

WHERE TO GET THE LOWDOWN ON MUTUAL FUNDS

Wouldn't it be great if someone could tell you which mutual funds are the good ones and which funds to avoid? Well, someone can—sort of. There are unbiased organizations that rank and rate mutual funds with the investor's best interests in mind. One of the best is a rating service called Morningstar, which is held in high esteem by money experts and consumer advocates. Most of Morningstar's ratings information is free on the web site www.morningstar.com.

The problem with any ratings service, including Morningstar, is that they can only tell you how a certain mutual fund has done in the past—not how it will do in the future. There's a standard saying on Wall Street that goes like this: *Past performance is not an indicator of future results.* So when you read that a particular stock mutual fund gets a high rating at Morningstar, all it means is that the fund did well in the past. Many funds did very well during the tech boom of the late 90's, for instance, only to have disastrous results when the tech bubble burst. So don't for a minute think that Morningstar can tell you which mutual funds are going to produce good results in the days, weeks, or months to come.

Still, it's always a good idea to do some research, especially if you're considering buying a managed fund. Among the kinds of information you can find at Morningstar are the following:

1. The name and biography of the fund's manager.

This is important if you're buying a managed fund, not so important for index funds. If you're going to put all your money into a fund where just one person decides how to spend it, you want to know something about his or her experience, track record, and background.

2. The fund's top 5 or 10 holdings.

You want to know what kinds of stocks this fund likes. Maybe they're buying a particular car company you hate, for instance. Or maybe they own a lot of technology stock, and you happen to think tech stocks are going to take a dive again. Find out what the mutual fund owns before you invest in it.

3. A short description of what kind of fund it is.

Is it a large cap fund? An aggressive growth fund? A balanced fund or a blend?

Morningstar rates funds using a star system. Five stars is their highest rating and one star their lowest. However, Morningstar cautions you not to consider solely the star rating when making financial choices. In the past, many five star funds have dropped to one or two star ratings over time. Instead, Morningstar advises you to look at how long a fund has been in business. If the return of the fund compares well to the average of competing funds over a period of 5 or 10 years, and if the return of the fund compares well to the index in its category, it's probably a superior fund.

Past performance is not an indicator of future results.

There are several good ways to buy mutual funds.

Direct Purchase

Many fund companies, or fund "families" as they're often called, will allow you to buy shares directly. If you know which fund you want to buy, you can log onto the company's web site or call their toll-free number.

Discount Brokerage

It's easy—and free—to buy no-load mutual funds through discount brokerage firms such as Charles Schwab, Ameritrade, or E-Trade. Many discount brokers offer various no-load funds and index funds to choose from. If you're determined to buy a fund that charges a load, and the fund doesn't offer direct purchase, you'll have to buy it from a brokerage firm that offers it. (Not all brokers offer every fund available.) For more on how to open a brokerage account, see Page 41.

Workplace 401(k)s

If your employer offers you a 401(k) retirement account or something similar, you'll be able to buy mutual funds that way. Many 401(k)s offer at least one index fund as a choice. (Do we have to say it again? Index funds are the safe way to go.)

HUH? WHAT'S THE PRICE?

Since the value of mutual funds depends on the price of a variety of stocks, all regular mutual funds are priced only once a day—at the close of trading. Practically speaking, this means that when you buy a mutual fund, you don't really know what price you'll pay because the price isn't set until the stock market closes. The same is true for selling—which makes it tricky. Do you want to sell all 1,000 shares of a fund that was priced at $20 a share when the market closed yesterday—even though the price might only be $15 today? But hey, if you wait until the market closes to find out that the price went up to $22 a share, whoops—you've missed your chance to sell it at that price. If you place the order to sell it tomorrow, who knows what the price will be?

EXCHANGE TRADED FUNDS

One way to avoid the frustration of not knowing the price of the mutual fund until after you've bought or sold it is to go for a new product called Exchange Traded Funds, or ETF's. These are a lot like index funds, except that they're bought and sold like stocks, which means two things: 1) you'll pay a commission or fee for the trade and, 2) you can buy and sell them throughout the day—so you actually know the price when you're buying or selling. Sounds good? Well, that part is, but the bottom line is that the fees and commissions you pay to buy or sell ETF's can outweigh the benefits.

The one exception would be an ETF that represents a special area of the market that isn't available elsewhere. For instance, the Nasdaq 100 is a collection of 100 tech stocks which you can buy or sell throughout the trading day as if it's a single stock. Some investors have found it advantageous to be able to buy and sell ETF's based on the way the market is performing at a given moment. (If this sounds suspiciously like day trading—the practice of buying and selling stocks throughout the day, hoping to make a profit as the prices rise and fall—it is. Be afraid. Be very afraid.)

> **Some investors buy and sell ETF's based on the way the market is performing at a given moment. If this sounds suspiciously like day trading, it is. Be afraid. Be very afraid.**

One of the smartest things you can do as an investor is put yourself on a schedule and just continue to buy shares of whatever mutual fund you've chosen, at regular intervals, no matter what. Repeat: no matter what.

This is called "dollar cost averaging," and it's great for two reasons. First, it's a system that keeps you from reacting emotionally to highs and lows in the market. If the market goes up, you might think to yourself, "I'm not going to buy now—it's too expensive." So you wait, and guess what? The price goes even higher! Then you buy, and of course the next day the price drops to an all-time low.

Trying to "time the market"—which is what it's called when you try to figure out when to get in and out—is a recipe for disaster. Very few people have success at that, and huge numbers of people fail. Instead, you dollar cost average by buying once a month (or at whatever interval you choose) no matter what the price. Naturally, the shares will be more expensive when the market is up, and less expensive when it's down. Over a period of time, however, these highs and lows average out, reducing your risk. In the long run, you'll very likely pay less per share than if you'd tried to jump in and out of the market based on gut instinct, emotion, a hot tip, or the phases of the moon. And your average cost per share will be lower—which means you make more money. That's the whole idea, isn't it?

35

BUY! SELL!

TAKING STOCK OF STOCKS

Why would anyone want to get "mauled" in the stock market? Why take the risk?

If you've ever seen the floor of the New York Stock Exchange on TV, you know what a wild, energetic, and exciting scene it can be. People are shouting at each other, running around, and waving their arms. It seems like utter chaos—and for a lot of people, that's the rush. They like the thrill of the hunt, the buzz they get when they think about making a "killing" and getting rich overnight. And yes, once in a while it happens that way. But just as often, you can "lose your shirt" and go broke the next day since stocks can go up in value quickly and drop just as rapidly.

If you're a newcomer to the stock market, you'll need to get acquainted with some grizzly terminology. For instance, when there's a downturn in the market it's called a "bear market." When stocks are riding high, it's a "bull market." Where did these vicious animal terms come from? Some people say it originated from the contrasting fighting styles of these two beasts. Bulls tend to attack upward with their horns. Bears swoosh down on an enemy or victim with their paws. Ouch.

Why would anyone want to get "mauled" in the stock market? Why take the risk? The answer is simple. Over the years, investors on average do better in stocks than in any other form of investment. In a 75 year period, from 1925–2002, stocks earned more than a 10% return on investment. And that includes the deep dark years of 1929 when the stock market crashed. If you leave out the crash of '29, the return for stocks since 1960 to the present has been even better. These return numbers reflect the average performance of large company stocks—the S&P 500 index. With such an impressive track record, financial planners urge small investors to simply bet on history repeating itself and purchase an index fund instead of trying to "beat the market." See more about mutual funds on Page 27.

5 RULES FOR CHOOSING STOCKS

Okay, okay. We've told you repeatedly to simply buy a mutual fund and be done with it—yet here you are, still reading this chapter about how to buy stocks. Well, if you're totally determined to get into individual stock purchases, here are some sensible rules for buying both individual stocks and mutual fund stocks.

1. BUY ONLY WHAT YOU KNOW AND UNDERSTAND.

Don't invest your life savings on a "hot tip" you heard about a stock or mutual fund. Hot tips usually lead to big losses. Know what you are buying into. And remember that investing is common sense. If an investment does not make sense to you, no matter who is telling you otherwise, steer clear of it.

remember this?

2. DON'T BUY JUST BECAUSE A STOCK IS "UP" IN VALUE.

Too often consumers buy a stock at its peak and then watch it drop. Frustrated that they are losing money, they sell the stock when it's near its lowest point. This is called the "buy high-sell low" mistake. The trick is to do just the opposite—buy low and sell high. But that takes patience, lots of homework, and enough money to survive a few mistakes.

3. DIVERSIFY!

This is a fancy word which means spread your money around. Many investors bought up only high tech stocks in the 1990's, for instance. That was a smart move for a while, but then high tech stocks plunged and those investors lost everything. Smart investors diversify, buying a variety of stocks. This is one of the continuing appeals of mutual funds.

4. BUY STOCKS OF COMPANIES THAT ARE FINANCIALLY STRONG.

If they have plenty of cash on hand and very low debt, these companies are likely to survive a recession or a bear market.

5. DON'T LET YOUR EMOTIONS RUN AWAY WITH YOU.

Too many stock investors are motivated by two powerful emotions—greed and fear. Either one can warp your judgment and cause you financial misery. Use your head and not your heart when making financial decisions.

If you're baffled by the letters and numbers that crawl across the bottom of the screen on financial TV networks, check out this quick key to the ticker.

| NYSE | HD 32 | IBM 91.20 | GE 25.60 | SFA 31 |
| NASDAQ & AMEX | MSFT 25 | INTC 26 | ORCL 11.40 | JDSU 4.23 |

THERE ARE TWO ROWS OF SYMBOLS.

The top row represents stocks traded on the New York Stock Exchange (NYSE). The bottom row is for stocks traded on the NASDAQ and the American Stock Exchange (AMEX).

THE LETTERS STAND FOR A SPECIFIC COMPANY'S STOCK.

For instance, Microsoft is MSFT. Home Depot is HD. IBM is… IBM! (Big surprise.) You can look up the ticker symbols online at www.nyse.com.

ABOUT THE COLORS

Red symbols mean the stock price is lower than it was when the market closed the day before. Green means the price is up. Blue or white means the price is unchanged. Yellow stands for a trade made "after hours."

Some tickers show just the symbol and price. Others have more info, as follows:

MSFT 15K@ 25.03 ▼ 0.16

| Ticker Symbol | Shares Traded | Price Traded | Change Direction | Change Price |

Translated: a trade just happened. Someone sold 15,000 shares of Microsoft at $25.03— down 16 cents from the previous closing price the day before. These letters are in red because the price is lower.

Every so often, you'll see the top or bottom row cluttered up with some additional numbers—the market summary. For more details and an explanation, visit www.realuguides.com.

THE DOW

The Dow Jones Industrial Average, or the Dow for short, is an index of the stock prices of 30 major industrial companies. The number used today isn't really an average, but it nonetheless reflects the overall strength or weakness of those 30 companies in the market. When the group as a whole does well, the Dow is up. When the group does poorly, the Dow is down. For more about the Dow, visit www.realuguides.com.

HOW TO OPEN A
BROKERAGE ACCOUNT

1 **Decide whether you want
a discount broker or a full service broker.**

Discount brokerage companies

Discount brokerage companies will let you open an account that is
controlled by you and no one else. You make all the decisions with this
kind of account. Commissions to buy or sell stock will be lower because
you aren't paying anyone to manage the account for you. For a list of
some of the best-known discount brokers with links to their web sites,
go to www.realuguides.com.

Full service brokers

Full service brokers require that a sales person open your account and also
help you select your stocks and provide advice. This person receives a part
of the commission you pay when you buy and sell stocks. The commission
is usually much higher than a discount brokerage firm would charge. Think
carefully about full service brokers. While many full service brokers are hon-
est people who do a good job for clients, there are many others who will
pressure you to trade just to make another commission. There's an inherent
conflict of interest in full service brokerage firms because the broker makes
more money if you buy and sell frequently. They also make more money
if you buy load mutual funds rather than no-load. If you hire a full service
broker, make sure you understand how that person is compensated. Also
make sure you're confident that the advice you're getting is worth the price.

2 **Find out what the minimum deposit required is.**

A few brokerage firms will let you open an account with a small amount of
money—as little as $500. However, most of the best known discount brokers
have minimums ranging from $2,000 to $10,000.

3 **Visit the brokerage firm's office,
call their toll free number, or check out their web sites
for information about how to sign up online.**

You can often handle the initial deposit by mail if you don't live near
a brokerage firm's branch office.

FULL SERVICE BROKERS: ARE THEY EVER WORTH IT?

Why would you need a full service broker? If you don't trust your own judgment in the market, you might want someone to manage your account for you. Remember, though, that most good brokers want their clients to be involved in the decision making process. You should never simply hire a full service broker and then relinquish all responsibility for the investments, hoping that the broker will handle your money well. That's taking more of a risk than any investor should take!

A PIECE OF ADVICE

Sure, reading this book is a good start. But the day may come when you need a bit more financial advice, and you'll want to consult a living, breathing human being—or at least someone with a pulse. Consumer advocates urge you to shop for a good financial advisor, and choose only those who are fee-only advisors—those who work on an hourly basis or who collect a fee based on a percentage of the money you invest. (Stay away from advisors who earn commissions from the investments they recommend—it's that conflict of interests thing again.) It's a good idea to interview at least two or three planners and then choose the one with the best qualifications.

You can find links to lists of fee-only advisors at www.realuguides.com.

OTHER WAYS TO BUY STOCKS

If you don't have enough cash to open an account, you can still purchase stocks and get into the market with just a few dollars. Here are two opportunities:

NO-LOAD STOCK PROGRAMS

Many companies offer "direct purchase" programs that allow investors to send in a small amount of money on a regular basis to purchase shares of that company's stock. To find out if the stock you're interested in is available this way, call the company's corporate headquarters and speak to someone in their Investor Relations department. Ask if they have a no-load stock program, and if so, ask to enroll in it. Some firms also provide this information on their web site.

buy her a share in her favorite bicycle company

ONE SHARE PROGRAMS

Although most companies have stopped issuing stock certificates these days, you can still buy a single share of stock for yourself through www.oneshare.com, and have the actual paper certificate mailed to you. This is more of a novelty than an investment, because the price for one share sold this way is much higher than the actual market price. But it's a great way to have fun and give a great gift to a friend or family member. If your biker buddy rides a Harley motorcycle, you can buy him a share of Harley Davidson stock for his birthday and have the stock certificate framed. Hundreds of companies sell one-share stocks through web sites such as www.oneshare.com or giveashare.com.

Bonds aren't the most glamorous investment you can make, but they are generally dependable and safe.

BONDING WITH BONDS

If many people find stocks sexy, they often find bonds downright boring. Where's the excitement, the thrill of making a lot of money overnight? O.K., so bonds aren't the most glamorous investment you can make, but they aren't the worst thing you could do with your money, either. Bonds are generally dependable and safe, and some U.S. government bonds known as TIPS are a good hedge against inflation. As you get older and closer to retirement, "safe" will start sounding pretty good to you. But it's also fine to start using bonds when you're younger, to diversify your portfolio.

WHAT ARE BONDS?

A bond represents an agreement by you to lend your money to a company or the government. The bond is issued at a set price with a promise that you'll get your money back at the end of a period of time. That's assuming, of course, that the company or government issuing the bond is still financially strong when the time's up, which is usually a safe bet—but don't buy bonds from any company or government that seems iffy on this issue.

How does it work? Let's say you buy a ten-year bond from a company at 5% for $10,000. Each year for a 10-year period you get $500 in interest. At the end of ten years the company sends back the principal, your original $10,000. Now you've got $15,000. Still bored?

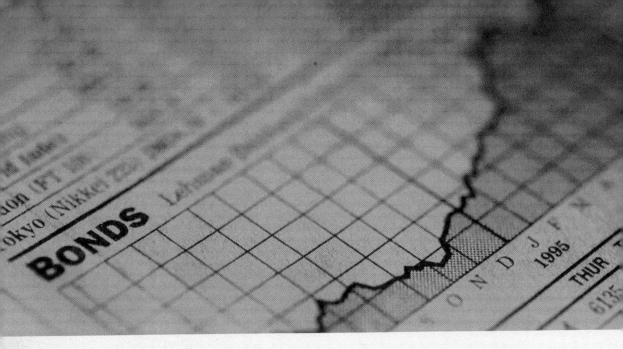

TYPES OF BONDS

Bonds come in every shape and size. Here are a few of the most familiar ones:

CORPORATE BONDS

Corporate bonds are backed by the company that issues them and carry a promise that you get your money back at the end of the stated period in the bond.

CONVERTIBLE BONDS

Convertible bonds are issued by a company, but it agrees to pay you back later in company stock equal to the amount of cash you invested.

MUNICIPAL BONDS

Municipal bonds are issued by U.S. towns, cities and states. They are popular because the interest is generally free from income tax if you live in the same state where the bond was issued.

The interest from municipal bonds is usually free from income tax.

U.S. GOVERNMENT SECURITIES

U.S. government securities are issued with the full faith and credit of the U.S. Treasury. They are considered the safest income investments in the world.

U.S. GOVERNMENT AGENCY BONDS

U.S. government agency bonds are issued by organizations associated with government programs. The best known are the bonds of mortgage agencies that are backed by a giant pool of mortgages such as Fannie Mae. These are not, however, backed by the U.S. Treasury, and are not considered quite as safe as U.S. Government securities.

FOREIGN GOVERNMENT BONDS

Foreign government bonds are issued (no surprise here) by foreign governments. Safe? Some are and some aren't, depending on the country.

WHAT ARE BONDS GOOD FOR?

We could talk about the bond market for the rest of this book and still hardly scratch the surface. However, what you need to know as a small investor is one simple fact: Bonds are generally appropriate for income and not for growth.

An investor who wants growth looks for investments that will increase in value over a long period of time. An investor who wants income wants investments that will pay off in the short term, providing money to live on. Bonds work best when you're relying on them for income, not long-term growth. The reason this is true is quite simple: Investments like stocks and real estate simply have a greater potential for growth over the long term than bonds. But bonds offer the security and predictability you want in a short-term investment—in fact, they're so predictable that you know exactly how much interest you're going to make when you buy them.

However, in a twist that is hard to fathom, bonds can occasionally "grow" and increase in value from time to time. How is this possible? When interest rates go down, the value of a bond bought in the past rises. Why? Because the interest rate of your bond is fixed. Thus if you buy a 5% bond and interest rates drop to 4%, your bond is still worth 5%. But the new bonds are being issued at the lower 4% rate—so your old bond is now worth more than the new ones. Consequently, you can cash in by selling your old bond for more than its original issue price. The higher price of your bond is the "growth" that bond traders are looking for in the market.

BOND FUNDS, NOT TO BE CONFUSED WITH BONDS

If you've checked out What Are Bonds Good For? on Page 47, you'll understand that bonds can occasionally grow —and where there's potential for growth, there are mutual funds. "Bond funds" are mutual funds made up entirely of bonds, which the fund managers try to trade at the right time to take advantage of bonds that have increased in value.

There are some advantages and disadvantages with bond funds, but the key point to remember is this: Investing in bond funds is not like investing in bonds —there are risks involved, just like with stock funds.

RISKS

A survey conducted in 2003 found that 70% of investors believed that a bond fund always guaranteed their principal or initial investment. This is a widespread misconception. Unlike an individual bond, a bond fund guarantees nothing, and there can be losses. As interest rates fluctuate, the value of the bonds in the fund can go down, so that your investment may be worth less from time to time.

BENEFITS

The primary benefit to investing in a bond fund is that it's less volatile than stock mutual funds. When the stock market is falling, bond funds tend to lose less money than all-stock mutual funds. Of course they also tend to make less when the stock market goes up. But overall, some investors feel safer with a mix of bond funds and mutual funds.

should we buy?

THE BOTTOM LINE ON BONDS

Safe? Boring? Or both? A good idea for a balanced portfolio? The truth is that you can easily develop a good portfolio without bonds or bond funds. Statistics have shown that you'll make more money in stocks, and if you want stability and some security in your portfolio, you can buy a few CD's or money market funds.

However, in situations in which you need to make a steady income over the short term from your investments—and retirement is a prime example—bonds can be an excellent and safe investment.

But don't overestimate bonds. The rule that bond funds will always go up when stocks go down is another misconception. While that's often been the case, there have been plenty of times when both stocks and bonds went down together. And there is no guarantee that bonds are going to do well in the future. No one has a crystal ball to predict that.

bonds are best for retirement income

49

FIRST STOP:

YOUR FUTURE

INVESTING FOR RETIREMENT

Retirement is your number one investment goal —well, either that or making mega-millions so you can buy a small country off the coast of South America.

But frankly, retirement is likely to happen sooner. And since these days people are often retired for 20, 30, or even 40 years, your retirement may turn out to be more expensive than owning that banana republic.

So how are you going to hang in there without a regular income years from now, when digital cable TV skyrockets to $300 a month, and movie tickets go for $20 a pop? Best answer: Invest in a retirement plan now. Here's a quick look at the various kinds of retirement plans you might run into. There are two main categories—plans you can join at work, and individual retirement accounts that you set up yourself.

30 years to go! ⟶

WORKPLACE INVESTMENT PLANS

These are retirement accounts that your employer sets up for you. Many times, your employer will make some of the contributions and you will make some. In the best plans, for every dollar you put into the account, the company matches it! That doubles your money—and with compound interest, it will grow even faster. Here are the basic types:

401(K) PLANS

Wouldn't it be great if 401K was the amount of money you'd have after you set up one of these plans? No such luck. 401(k) is the name of the IRS tax code section that these retirement accounts are based on. This is the most common kind of company-sponsored account. It lets you set up an automatic deduction from your paycheck before income taxes are deducted. That saves you big bucks because it means you won't have to pay taxes on the money you put into your retirement account. Not all 401(k)s are alike, so you'll have to get the details from your employer. But by law, they've got to give you some choices about where you can invest the money—at least three investment choices in addition to the company's own stock. Most 401(k) plans limit your choice of investments to mutual funds.

403(B) PLANS

Different numbers, but the same idea. These are basically 401(k) plans for employees of the government, schools, and non-profit institutions. In recent years, some 403(b)s have been replaced by the newer 401(k)s, but 403(b)s are still quite common. Technically, a 403(b) is called an annuity, which means that a specific income is periodically paid to you during retirement for a fixed number of years. Many experts are critical of annuities in general (often with good reason), but this one is different—this is one annuity that's definitely worth investing in, and for some employees it may be the only choice.

457 PLANS

These are sometimes called "deferred compensation" plans. As in other plans, money is invested before income taxes and paid out in retirement. For more info and links about 457's, visit www.realuguides.com.

SEP-IRA

SEP stands for Simplified Employee Pension, and IRA for Individual Retirement Account. If you work for a small business owner, he or she might offer this kind of plan because it allows the employer to make contributions to employees' retirement without being involved in a more complex plan. Like the 403(b), many SEP-IRA's are being phased out and replaced by 401(k) plans.

PENSION PLANS

There was a time in America when nearly everyone who had a job had some kind of pension plan provided by the company. But that was the old days when companies employed people for their whole working

I love my 401(k)!

lives. People change jobs more often now, and most pension plans have been disbanded in favor of the more flexible 401(k) which you can take with you from one job to another. In a pension plan it was the company that did the investing, guaranteeing you a monthly "paycheck" after you retired. Now you have to do more of the work of investing yourself, but the benefits can be even greater.

YOUR OWN RETIREMENT PLANS

Whether you're self-employed and salivating over these company retirement plans that you can't take advantage of—or just want to increase your retirement investing choices—there are lots of options for self-managed retirement plans. If you're self-employed, you may not get all those juicy matching dollars, or all the pre-tax incentives that are offered in 401(k)s, but your money can grow too. And even if you are employed, you may want to add a Roth IRA to your financial picture. Read on.

IRA

A tax deductible Individual Retirement Account (IRA) is the investment of choice for many self-employed people, and for many employees whose companies don't have another plan. It's flexible and allows you to make your own investment choices. But there are still rules you have to follow. For links to information about IRA's, visit www.realuguides.com.

SEP IRA

A SEP is like having your own 401(k) account if you work for yourself. It is a low-cost pension plan for the self-employed and small business employers. One of its advantages over a traditional IRA is that there is a higher limit of how much income you can put into it. Be careful though. If your little business grows and you hire employees, by law they have the right to be part of your SEP IRA, too.

ROTH IRA

In a traditional IRA, your yearly investment in the IRA is tax deductible. The newer Roth IRA doesn't allow for this deduction. However, unlike the traditional IRA, money drawn from the Roth IRA is tax-free! The rules for Roth accounts are somewhat complicated and continue to change. There are also restrictions on income levels for Roths. All the same, Roth IRA's are one of the best ways to invest for retirement, so read on.

10 years? Convert to ROTH! →

ALL ABOUT ROTH IRA'S

One of the fundamental rules of investing is that when you can legally avoid taxes, do it. Company retirement plans do this by delaying when you or your heirs pay taxes. The Roth IRA does it by letting you avoid taxes completely in the future. What could be better than that?

So who can put money into a Roth IRA? That depends. They aren't just for the self-employed, however. If you take part in a company retirement plan like a 401(k), you may still be allowed to put money into a tax-free Roth IRA. While the Roth IRA was more restrictive previously, the new law on Roth says anyone can open one if she has earned income below a certain level. Those limits (as of 2004) are:

FOR SINGLE TAX FILERS:
Income up to $95,000
(to quality for a full contribution)

From $95,000 to $110,000
(for a partial contribution)

FOR JOINT FILERS:
Income up to $150,000
(for a full contribution)

From $150,000 to $160,000
(for a partial contribution)

Note that the figures above refer to your Adjusted Gross Income, not your salary or total earned wages. For a complete explanation of full and partial contributions—and links to excellent web sites with more info about Roth IRA's—visit www.realuguides.com.

TO CONVERT OR NOT CONVERT?

Conversion to a Roth IRA may be appropriate if:	**Leaving assets in a traditional IRA may be appropriate if:**
You have 10 or more years to save until retirement	You have fewer than 10 years to save until retirement
You have enough money outside your IRA to pay the taxes	You will need to tap your retirement account to pay the taxes on a conversion
Your adjusted gross income is less than $100,000	Your adjusted gross income is more than $100,000
You expect to be in the same or higher tax bracket when you retire	You expect to be in a lower tax bracket when you retire

THE ROTH STRATEGY

If the Roth IRA is sounding better and better, but you're already investing in a 401(k) at work, what are you supposed to do? Never fear—there's a Roth strategy that allows you to have the best of both worlds. Simply continue putting money into your company retirement plan "up to the match." In other words, if the company will give you 50 cents for every dollar you put into your plan, up to the first 3% of your salary, then contribute up to the 3%. Any money you would have put in beyond that point can be allocated to a tax-free Roth instead. The income restrictions may change in the future along with the contribution limits, so check the rules each year with your accountant.

CONVERTING TO A ROTH IRA

You may be thinking, "Gee, this Roth IRA sounds so good, I think I'll convert more of my retirement portfolio to a Roth." This is a lot easier said than done. First, there are income limits that prevent some people from converting. Second, you will have to pay income taxes on the amount you convert just as you would with a traditional IRA distribution. Be careful. You can't take the money from the "converting IRA" to pay the taxes without paying a penalty. It is considered an early distribution from an IRA if you are under 59½ years old. This means the amount you take out is subject to an additional 10% tax penalty on top of regular taxes. Ouch! Consider the chart on Page 54 before converting.

THE JOYS OF TAX-SHELTERED COMPOUNDING

Investing before taxes is clearly the way to go. But don't take our word for it. Take a look at this chart.

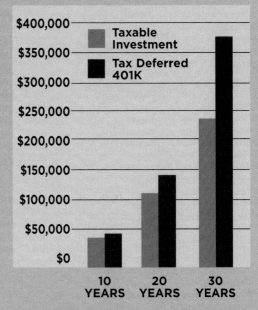

In the chart, a person puts $250 each month into a 401(k) to make an average return of 8% a year. Compare that to the very same amount going into a taxable investment assuming a 27% income tax rate. The chart says it all. A long-term retirement plan builds your money fast and easy. When the time comes for you to switch over from growth to income investments, you'll have a nice big nest egg. You can live off the interest of your investments without touching the principal. Now that's living large!

55

HOW TO MAKE A MILLION DOLLARS

Forget the TV game shows, bypass the lottery, and never mind trying to become the next American Idol. Here's what it takes to retire with a million dollars the easy way—by investing. As always, the sooner you start, the better. Below is a chart showing how much money you will have to invest each year—depending on your age when you start socking it away—in order to have at least one cool million when you retire at age 65.

These figures assume that you'll get a 9% average annual return and that you put the money into a tax deferred investment.
Note that if you start after you are 45 years old, you can't get to a million bucks in your company retirement plan, due to tax laws that limit contributions to those kinds of accounts.

Age 20	$136/month	or	$1,902/year
Age 25	$214/month	or	$2,960/year
Age 30	$340/month	or	$4,636/year
Age 35	$547/month	or	$7,337/year
Age 40	$892/month	or	$11,807/year
Age 45	$1498/month	or	$19,547/year

And if you want to give a gift to a newborn, put away $2,000 when he is born. He will have $541,692 when he retires at age 65. Put $3,963 into a tax-deferred account making an average 9% a year, and he will have a cool million!

HOW MUCH SHOULD YOU INVEST?

Here's the simple truth about saving and investing for retirement—the sooner you start, the less you have to put away. An amazing example that proves this point can be seen on the opposite page which demonstrates the following: If you invest monthly for ten years—from the age of 18 until you're 28—*and then never invest another penny again*, you'll have more money at retirement than if you'd saved the same amount each month starting at age 28 and kept doing it until you retired at age 65!

Of course, the best plan is to sock away some money every month from now on, so that you'll really be living easy during your retirement years. How much? Think ten percent of your monthly salary if you're in your 20's or 30's. If you're older and have put off starting for too long, you'll have to raise that figure to make up for lost time and income. Again, it's not how much you save but how soon you get started that will determine whether you'll be able to retire in comfort.

For a more specific calculation on how much you actually need to invest for your circumstances, go to www.realuguides.com and check out our retirement calculator.

MAX & MEREDITH: A COMPARISON

MAX

Max wanted to live the good life when he was young. He spent $200 a month on beer, movies, clubs, clothes, and expensive dinners in his teens and early twenties. Then suddenly it hit him: He needed to start saving for retirement. So when he turned 28, he started investing that $200 a month in a tax-sheltered fund that earned 9% on average each year. If he keeps putting in $200 a month for the next 37 years—until he retires at age 65— he'll have $709,156.

MEREDITH

Meredith was more careful with her money when she was young. She went out with friends only once or twice a month. At age 18, she started investing $200 a month in the same fund Max chose, earning 9% on average each year. At age 28, she stopped investing. Now that she's married and about to have kids, she needs that extra $200 a month for her new family expenses. So for the next 37 years, she'll never invest another penny! But guess what? Because she started earlier, Meredith will have more money at age 65 than Max will—an impressive $938,696. And she only had to invest for 10 years instead of 37!

EDUCATION

If you think your college education was expensive, just wait until you see what it's going to cost your kids!

They say only two things in life are certain—taxes, and the snowballing ascendance to power of blonde, marginally talented pop stars. In truth, you could add a few other things to this list: the maligning of Brussels sprouts, stand-up comedy bits about airline food, and, perhaps most pertinent to our current subject, the rising cost of a college education.

Yeah, that's right: If you think *your* college education was expensive, just wait until you see what it's going to cost your kids! (Talk about sticker shock.) The average cost of college for the 2003–2004 school year, including tuition, fees, room and board (and calls home begging for more money) was about $4,694 at an in-state public university and $19,710 at a private school, according to the College Board. But the more selective private colleges can run closer to $27,000, and some of the most expensive schools even go above $35,000 a year. And that's just this year. By next year, costs will be up by about 6%, says the ever-cheery College Board.

The bottom line is that you can't start that college fund too soon—in fact, it

might seem like you can't start it soon enough. Luckily, there are three different ways of saving and investing for college.

- The 529 Savings Plan

- The Coverdell ESA

- Gifts to a child's custodial account

Turn the page for the lowdown on each of these college savings techniques.

How much will her college education cost?

The 529 Savings Plan is a state-sponsored college savings plan. It is the only college savings plan that is completely tax-free, regardless of income.

In a 529 Plan you can invest for education in both mutual funds and fixed interest accounts. You don't get a deduction for saving in a 529 plan, but the earnings are tax-free as long as it is spent exclusively on a child's higher education—which could mean either a four-year college, trade school, or graduate school. The cash can also be applied toward college related expenses, like books, equipment, fees, and some room and board expenses.

There is one catch, however. Congress has allowed "tax-free" exemption to the 529 plans only through 2010. After that date, lawmakers will have to renew the exemption or the plan returns to its original form, which wasn't so bad either. Under those rules, money removed in later years for college education was taxed at the student's lower tax rate rather than the higher tax rate of the adult custodian, the person who actually opened the account.

There is one new, independent, private 529 savings plan, and there are 50 state-sponsored 529 plans—one for each state.

This doesn't mean you have to buy the plan from your state—shop around, and if you find a plan in another state that offers a better deal, go for it. Since you don't have to attend school in the state where you invested money in the plan, there's no reason not to shop around and check out different states' plans.

But since determining which state's plan is the best can be a little tricky, or at the very least time-consuming, you may want to check out some other resources. Visit www.realuguides.com for links to sites with excellent advice.

The cash from 529 plans can also be applied toward college related expenses, like books, equipment, fees, and some room and board expenses.

Here are some more advantages to 529 plans:

- The state where you live may give you a state tax deduction for money you contribute to a 529 plan.

- Most plans allow deposits of as little as $25 or as much as $200,000 to start making them great for people of all income levels.

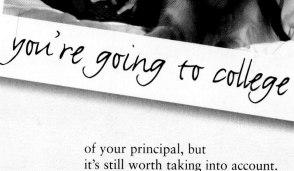

you're going to college

- Most plans have an automatic deposit feature, which makes it easy to invest every month.

- If you don't like one plan after you join it, you can transfer to any other plan.

- If one child doesn't use all the money in the plan, you can change the beneficiary so the balance goes to another child. That child doesn't have to be your own child, but can be any legal relative, such as a niece or nephew. You can even make yourself the beneficiary if you want to go back to school.

The 529 Plan may be extremely flexible, but it does have a few rules you'll want to consider. Here are the most important ones:

- If you decide to use the money in a 529 plan for non-educational purposes, you pay a penalty of 10% of your profit. This isn't a huge loss, considering that you get back 100% of your principal, but it's still worth taking into account.

- Some plans include various fees which can add up to quite an expense. Shop around before you sign up. Check out www.realuguides.com for more info.

- You must disclose all money held in a 529 Plan when you apply for financial aid. It might affect that application, but experts insist it is still better than the old method of a gift account to a minor.

- You can transfer an old gift account for a minor (also known as a "custodial plan") to many 529 plans, but to do so, you've got to sell the old account's investments and set up a new "custodial" 529 Plan. Not all states allow this kind of transfer of funds into their 529 Plans, so look around.

COVERDELL ESA

Formerly known as the Educational IRA, this college savings plan got a makeover and a new name: the Coverdell ESA. If you qualify as a parent within the income limits, you can set up a Coverdell ESA (Educational Savings Account). Unlike a 529 Plan, money in a Coverdell can be taken out at any time for any legitimate educational need, including tuition at a private elementary, middle or high school.

Here's how it works:

■ Annual donations to a Coverdell ESA are not tax deductible, but withdrawals of any earnings are tax-free as long as the money is spent on a child's education.

■ Anyone can set up a Coverdell ESA for any child through a bank, mutual fund company, or brokerage firm. You can choose any investment you want through any of these outlets.

■ The combined contribution to any one child is limited to $2,000 a year.

■ Money in a Coverdell can be used for nearly any education-related expense, including a computer.

■ Money in a Coverdell, as with a 529 Plan, must be reported when you're applying for financial aid, and may affect the financial aid package you're offered.

■ The annual income of the parents determines whether you can open a Coverdell or not. See where you fit into this chart:

If you file your tax form:	Your adjusted gross income is:	Then this is what you can contribute to a Coverdell ESA
Single	Less than $95,000	$2,000 per child per year
	$95,000 to $110,000	Partial contribution permitted
	More than $110,000	No contribution permitted
Married, filing jointly	Less than $190,000	$2,000 per child per year
	$190,000 to $220,000	Partial contribution permitted
	More than $220,000	No contribution permitted

GIFTS

Getting your grandmother to fork over a chunk of change to finance your college education is certainly the simplest way to "save" for college. But there are other advantages to this rather blunt investment that you and your grandma may not have thought of.

For example, if your grandparent gives you shares of a stock purchased years ago, the grandparent doesn't pay taxes on the profit made from the stock. You pay the tax in your tax bracket when you sell the stock—and if you're a student or have a low income, you may be in a much lower bracket than Granny was! The savings in taxes can be extraordinary. In fact, if you time it right and the tax laws don't change, you could end up paying zero federal taxes using this technique. New tax laws go into effect on January 1, 2008, and today's lowest tax bracket (5%) will drop to zero. If you can wait until 2008 to start making big money, and you are in the lowest tax bracket, you could qualify for major savings when you cash out your gift stocks.

But what if the law changes between now and then? Gifting was always a wise investment strategy for college before the laws made it even better, but at the same time, it is a shadowy area with lots of rules and regs. So make sure grandma and grandpa (or parents, aunts, uncles, second cousins, etc.) consult a good tax advisor before they fork over any stocks to the college fund.

There is one other problem with gifts. Once the gift is made, the giver can't control how it's used. If your allegedly college-bound nephew wants, he can sell the stock, buy himself a flashy sports car, and head west. This is obviously not a problem with 529 Plans, in which adult custodians control the account at all times.

HOW MUCH DO I NEED TO SAVE?

As always, when you start saving is much more important than how much you save. And to illustrate the point further, you can check out this table below, which shows how much money would be saved if parents saved a small amount ($10 to $50) every week in a tax-sheltered college savings program:

Weekly	0% for 17 years	5% for 17 years
$10	$8,840	$13,888
$25	$22,100	$34,722
$50	$44,200	$69,445

If you want to find out how much you'll need to save for college education, use the calculator you will find online at www.realuguides.com.

MORE REAL U...
CHECK OUT THESE OTHER REAL U GUIDES!

YOUR FIRST APARTMENT
Whether you're leaving home for the first time, heading off to college...or skipping the college thing and sliding straight into a real job and real life, this guide has everything you need to know to move out of the house and start your life for real.

IDENTITY THEFT
Find out how to protect yourself from the #1 crime in the U.S. Includes expert advice about surfing the Internet without leaving a trail for the criminals to follow. From the world-renowned identity theft expert and subject of the blockbuster motion picture *Catch Me If You Can.*

BUYING YOUR FIRST CAR
Don't get burned on the first big purchase you make. Find out how to get the best financing, how to avoid the latest scam tactics, whether to buy extended warranties, and more.

FOR MORE INFORMATION ON THESE AND OTHER REAL U GUIDES, VISIT WWW.REALUGUIDES.COM.